Nautical *Knots* *and* Lines ILLUSTRATED

INTERNATIONAL MARINE
CAMDEN, MAINE

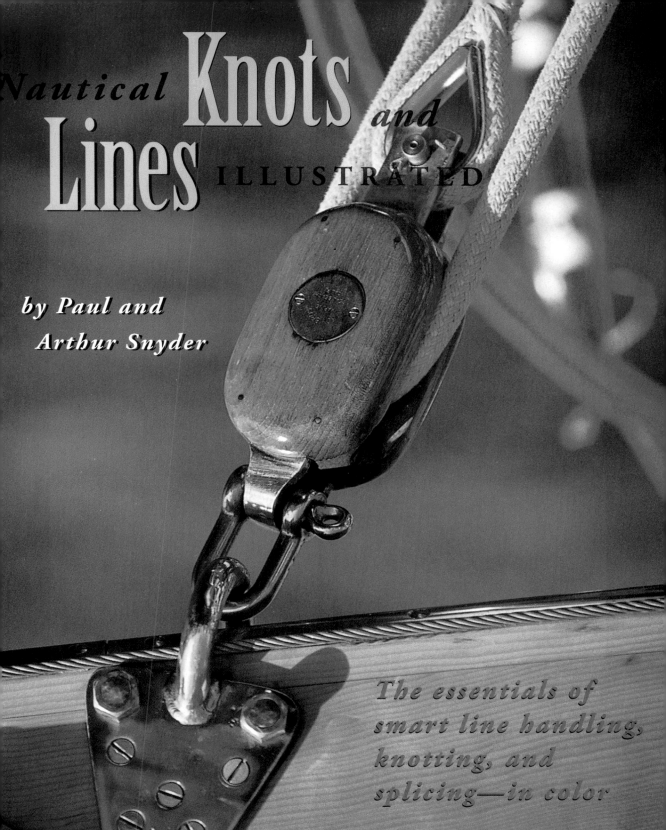

Nautical Knots and Lines Illustrated

by Paul and Arthur Snyder

The essentials of smart line handling, knotting, and splicing—in color

Acknowledgments

We wish to thank

J. Lars White for his advice and

photographers Carl Andrews, Craig Dripps, and Billy Black.

Many boats and locations were used, in particular:

Concordia Boat Company, Brodie MacGregor, owner;

Constitution Marina, Bob Davidoff, co-owner;

the Concordia yawl *Malay*, Dan Strohmeier, owner;

the J/130 *Sacajawea*, Grant McCargo II, owner.

International Marine/
Ragged Mountain Press
A Division of The *McGraw-Hill Companies*

2 4 6 8 10 9 7 5 3

Library of Congress Information
Snyder, Paul.
Nautical Knots & lines illustrated. Paul and Arthur Snyder.
p. cm.
ISBN 0-07-059580-1
1. Knots and splices. 2 Cordage. I. Snyder, Arthur. II. Title.
VM533.S653 1996   96-5718
623.88'82--dc20   CIP

Questions regarding the ordering of
this book should be addressed to:

International Marine, P.O. Box 220,
Camden, ME 04843

Questions regarding the ordering of
this book should be addressed to:

The McGraw-Hill Companies
Customer Service Department
P.O. Box 547; Blacklick, OH 43004
Retail customers: 1-800-262-4729
Bookstores: 1-800-722-4726

Typeset in Adobe Serifa, Birch, and Garamond.
Printed by R.R. Donnelley, Willard, OH
Design by Design Associates
Edited by Jonathan Eaton, John Vigor
Production by Molly Mulhern, Dan Kirchoff,
and Mary Ann Hensel

Introduction

The primary purpose of this book is to teach the beginner how to tie the basic knots required on board sailboats and motorboats, specifically how to learn the motion that the hands go through to create the knot. This is fun for the beginner to learn and the sailor to teach.

Another purpose is to serve as a ready reference for those who have forgotten for the moment how to tie a certain knot, or for those old salts who learned a different way—"different ships, different long splices." For those who love the sea, working with knots is a great pleasure. A proper knot is satisfying, a poorly tied one embarrassing. Modern gear does eliminate some knots, but when something goes wrong, the correct knot often saves the day.

Practice, patience, and study enable the sailor to "see" the knot in the mind's eye. Then it can be tied with the eyes closed and it will be there when needed.

If it's available, study with two four-foot lengths of half-inch (12 mm) diameter rope of different materials. Almost any size of cord may be used, but half-inch provides the ability to feel and control the ropes while practicing.

Work slowly at first. The main objective is control, not speed. The difference between slow and fast is not worth retying. With a few controlled motions, the procedure is easily remembered. Ultimately, it is done by rote.

Most knots are worked with the hands, not with the fingers. Don't use your fingertips to push one line through a small loop in the other line. Tie the knot big enough so the hands hold the ropes. Construct the knot first, then work it down to size.

Marlinespike seamanship, fancy knotwork, and many splices, while they serve the mariner well, are mostly done while in dock or ashore, not underway. Our concern here is with the ropework skills that can save one's bacon or make one's reputation every day and night on the water.

One more note: Throughout the book, RH means right hand and LH means left hand. We show the knots from a right-hander's perspective, on the theory that left-handers are made more adaptable by a lifetime of experience.

Contents

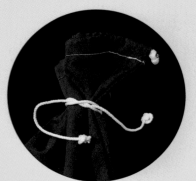

Synthetic Fibers Used in Rope

Natural-fiber ropes—manila, sisal, and hemp—have been replaced with synthetic fibers. The improvements are vast—the synthetic fibers are stronger, more durable, and don't swell and jam when they're wet. They are less abrasive, and more resistant to abrasion themselves. Many are impervious to water. Some synthetics are torque-balanced, so that they resist kinking or twisting when coiled. Synthetics are, however, affected by sunlight in varying degrees.

There are many options. The following are the major ones. Pages 12 and 13 show some of the ways rope is constructed from these fibers:

NYLON. Strong and stretchy, this fiber is favored for docking lines and anchor rodes, where its stretchiness is an advantage.

POLYESTER. Tradenames include Dacron and Terylene. Although Dacron is Dupont's trademark, it has become generic. This is a strong, low-stretch fiber that has excellent resistance to abrasion and sunlight. It is the most popular choice for running rigging.

HIGH-MODULUS POLYETHYLENE, OR SPECTRA. This high-tech rope is many times stronger than wire for the same weight. It floats, has low stretch, and resists abrasion. It does not "fish-hook" or corrode, it is clean, and it's easy to handle. The cost is high, but it is an ideal replacement for wire in many uses, such as halyards on racing sailboats that will not tolerate stretch. It does have a low melting point. When combined with other fibers in rope construction, the result is less expensive than pure Spectra yet still compares favorably to wire in strength. For example, rope with a Spectra-aramid core and braided polyester cover is as strong as 7 x 19 wire of half the diameter; the rope stretches about the same and weighs less.

ARAMID. Dupont's aramid fiber is called Kevlar. This is a strong (even stronger than Spectra), low-stretch fiber that does not creep. Good for halyards, mooring lines and some running rigging applications, but expensive, and prone to internal abrasion, which reduces its life expectancy. It's also stiff and hard to work.

POLYPROPYLENE. This is a lightweight, floating fiber, about 60% as strong as Dacron. It is vulnerable to the sun and to abrasion and will melt from friction when eased on a winch under strain. It is sometimes used as a core with other fibers to minimize weight, but is not recommended for unblended use.

Rope Care and Safety

Care

Abrasion and sharp edges are ropes' worst ene-mies. Masthead exit slots should be checked for burrs and rough edges.

Cotter pins or circular clips in turnbuckles or blocks should be taped to prevent snagging.

Dirt and salt will cause premature wear of the tiny filaments in the rope. Running rigging should be rinsed periodically with fresh water. Ropes may be put in a mesh bag and washed with a gentle cycle in a washing machine. A little fabric softener may be added to the rinse cycle. Hang them up to dry. Do not use the dryer.

The process of wrapping line around winches and casting off over the top of winches puts twist into rope, which can make it prone to kinking and jamming in blocks. Severe twist will flatten the rope out of round, resulting in faster wear.

To get rid of twist, trail your sheets astern from one end while the boat is moving. Let halyards hang free at both ends.

Safety

The main concerns in handling rope are over-loading and local abrasion.

- **OVERLOADING. If a line parts, it recoils with amazing force. Anyone standing in front of or behind the line can be seriously injured.**
- **LOCAL ABRASION. Constant use in the same spot—a jam cleat, turning block, or chocks—will cause chafing and wear. Watch for the first signs, and swap the line end-for-end once, then replace.**

Inspect lines often and closely. Minor wear or damage can reduce strength more than is apparent.

Last, but not least, stand clear (as much as is possible) of any line that is under high load when passed through a turning block, such as the bight of a genoa sheet or a halyard that is turned by a deck block. If the block were to pull out, one could be injured or thrown overboard.

Rope Construction

Traditional rope is constructed with three strands turned to the right. This is called "twisted," "stranded," or "laid-up." But most modern ropes are "braided" and some are "plaited," which makes them soft and flexible.

Braided Lines

The most common braided ropes are made from the materials listed on Page 10. Here are the principal types.

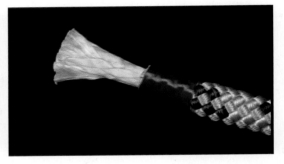

SINGLE BRAID. This photograph shows twelve-strand polyester rope, a blend of spun yarn (for pleasant handling) and filament (for durability and resistance to stretch). Its very supple construction absorbs twist to prevent kinking. It is excellent for frequently handled lines such as sheets, control lines, and furling lines. Filament nylon single braid is used for docking lines.

DOUBLE BRAID. This is the most common construction for running rigging, and has a braided core inside a braided cover. The core and cover contribute equally to the strength. Sometimes, however, the major strength comes from the core, with the cover acting as protection.

PARALLEL FIBER CORE. This is a bundle of unidirectional fibers surrounded by a braided cover. The parallel core results in less stretch and greater strength than the same size of double-braid line, making it perhaps the most popular choice for halyards. At first it is slightly stiffer than double braids, but it softens with use. The rope in this photo has a Spectra core and a polyester cover.

Stranded Lines

Today the most common stranded ropes are made up with three strands. Each strand has yarns twisted to the left. The strands themselves are twisted to the right to make the rope. "Cable" was made with three ropes twisted to the left and is now obsolete.

Stranded rope is made from these materials:

NYLON. It's easy to handle wet or dry, it knots and splices easily, and it is the most elastic of all ropes.

DACRON. This polyester spun-yarn rope is soft on the hands and economical, compared with braided line. It is used often by owners of classic boats because it feels similar to cotton and linen. It may be traditionally spliced or used in marlinespike seamanship, but it has less durability and resistance to stretch than filament line.

POLYPROPYLENE. The lightest and least expensive of all synthetic fibers. It produces low-stretch cordage, good for heaving lines, water-ski tow ropes, and life buoy lanyards. Sunlight degrades it, however, so it is not recommended for anchor rodes, dock lines, mooring lines, or running rigging. It is about 60 percent as strong as Dacron.

Explanation of Procedure

Procedure

For the knots and line-handling operations on the following pages, the camera has been located close to where your eye would be, and shows how things will look as you tie the knot. "To the rear" means "away from you," but in some pictures "up" might be more appropriate.

The initials RH and LH denote right hand and left hand.

Terms

The language of the sea will be used, as it has been for centuries. It is precise and picturesque. The Glossary defines terms with special nautical meaning, and also features a list of special line-handling commands.

A KNOT is formed in the line itself; for example, a Figure-of-Eight knot.
A BEND joins two lines; for example a Carrick Bend.
A HITCH bends a line to a spar, ring, or another line; for example, a Clove Hitch.

There are exceptions and contradictions, since seagoing terminology comes from different services and nations. As you read, practice with a piece of line so that you will become accustomed to the terminology.

If you're a novice, we suggest you begin with the uncomplicated Half Hitch, Figure-of-Eight, or Reef Knot. Learning to tie knots requires patience and persistence. Proceed one step at a time, making sure to follow the illustrations. A false step can be most frustrating since the knot cannot be tied.

END. The way we will use it, the last foot or two of the line. The Bitter End will be the last six inches of line.

NIP. The part or parts of the knot where the line itself or another line brings pressure to provide the friction that makes the knot hold. Nips on the better knots do not jam. A good knot may be untied as fast as it is tied.

and Terms Used

STANDING PART. The part of the line which leads from the knot being tied, toward the load.

BIGHT. A bend or loop in the line. A closed bight will signify that the line crosses itself in forming the bight. An open bight is formed when a loop is made without the line crossing itself.

A ROUND TURN. This full turn contacts the Fixed Object by more than 360 degrees. A Turn, by comparison, is a single wrap that reverses the direction of pull by 180 degrees.

SLACK. Looseness in a line. It may be in the knot itself or anywhere in the line. Also used as a verb.

Knots Used on Board

OVERHAND KNOT (left)
See Page 21
FIGURE-OF-EIGHT KNOT (center)
See Page 20

SINGLE HITCH
See Page 22

REEF KNOT
See Page 26

STEVEDORE KNOT
See Page 20

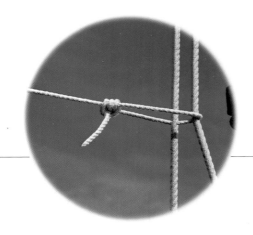

ROLLING HITCH
See Page 32

HALF HITCH
See Page 24

TWO HALF HITCHES
See Page 25

CLOVE HITCH (Crossing Knot)
See Page 28

CLOVE HITCH (Temporary)
See Page 30

Knots Used on Board <small>(CONTINUED)</small>

ROLLING HITCH
See Page 32

BOWLINE, around a Fixed Object
See Page 42

BECKET HITCH
See Page 34

CARRICK BEND
See Page 44

LASHING HITCH
See Page 52

STOWAGE COIL
See Page 68

SHEET BEND
See Page 38

BOWLINE, Fixed Loop
See Page 40

BOWLINE in a Bight (with a Becket Hitch
in the loop)
See Page 46

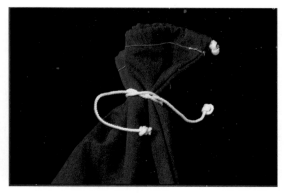

CONSTRICTOR KNOT
See Page 50

19

Figure-of-Eight

A practical and elegant stopper

To Tie...

1. With 5-inch end in RH, cross over Standing Part to the left, forming a Closed Bight.

2. Reach under Standing Part with RH and pull end under and around Standing Part. Bring up outside of Bight to the right.

3. With RH, tuck end back down through Closed Bight.

4. Work knot snug, adjusting length of end.

5. To add bulk, several Round Turns may be taken after Step 2. It is then called a Stevedore Knot.

Overhand Knot

The simplest and most basic stopper

Use...

- The first step in tying shoelaces.
- May be single, double (as shown here), or triple.
- Often used as a handhold in lifelines on life buoys, liferafts, and rescue boats.
- Makes a handy Stopper in the ends of whipping.

To Tie...

1. With a 12-inch end in RH, cross it over Standing Part in LH.

2. Bring end up through Bight. This is a Single Overhand Knot.

3. Take one more Round Turn and adjust length of end as needed.

4. Pull the ends sharply apart. This is a Double Overhand Knot. Work knot snug. For a Triple Overhand Knot, add one more turn at Step 3 above.

5. A Slipped Overhand Knot makes a temporary stopper, easily untied.

Making Fast to a Cleat

The correct (safe) way to belay a line

Many cleats are angled about 15 degrees to the lead of the Standing Part. With a "straight" cleat there is a tendency for the first turn to jam against the Standing Part. This is our recommended method to make fast.

To Tie...

1. Lead line on side of cleat that is angled away from the line, and to the far end of the cleat. Take only one Round Turn under both horns.

2. Cross over center of cleat with only one figure-eight turn.

5. This simple Hitch can be difficult to tie correctly in a hurry because you may be using either the left or the right horn of the cleat, and you may be using either the left or the right side of that horn to finish the Hitch. It all depends on the direction from which the line approaches the cleat, and it means four possible positions for starting the Hitch. Tying it the wrong way (as in this picture) puts the Standing Part along the side of the cleat rather than across the cleat, and the Nip is therefore weakened. The key is having the end on the correct side when forming the Single Hitch.

Use...

- A safe and economical way to belay any line to a cleat.
- Ensures easier control of the line when casting off and surging.
- Avoids jamming, holds securely, and releases instantly.

3. Make the line fast to the cleat with only a Single Hitch.

   Use your RH to lead the Standing Part to the left of the next horn as if another fig-ure-eight turn were being made, but stop with the end to the left of both horns—this is important. With your RH, make a small open Bight in the end. With your LH, twist the right side of the Bight to the left to make a Closed Bight. Drop it over horn.

4. Pull tight with your LH.

More Facts About Belaying

Remember: More than one Round Turn, one figure-eight turn, and one Single Hitch on a cleat are unseamanlike. Any more piled up on a cleat demonstrate nothing but insecurity.

   Incidentally, a line jammed on a cleat can endanger a boat. Make sure you know the preferred way to make fast for the boat you are on, and follow it without exception. Then, in the dark of the midwatch, there will be no surprises for anyone else casting off the line you secured.

Half Hitch

A simple form of the overhand knot

Use...

• Basis for several other knots.
• Used alone, it is not secure, and forms a temporary hitch only.

To Tie...

1. With RH, take a Turn around or through a Fixed Object with twelve inches of end. Hold Standing Part in LH.

2. With RH, pull end up and then to the left over Standing Part. Hold crossing with left thumb.

3. With RH, reach through Bight and pull end back through.

4. Pull up snug.

5. The Half Hitch is often slipped where quick untying is more important than security. Before the end is pulled through in Step 3 above, make a small bight in the end with RH, then pull this bight through the first bight. Shoe laces are "double" slipped.

Two Half Hitches

A simple, easily remembered knot

Use...

• Securing a line that will not be under great strain.
• Securing a line that will not shake until it comes loose.

To Tie...

1. Make a Half Hitch around a Fixed Object— see Page 24. With RH, pull end up and over Standing Part to the left. Hold end and Standing Part with left thumb and forefinger.

2. With RH, reach through Bight and pull end back through.

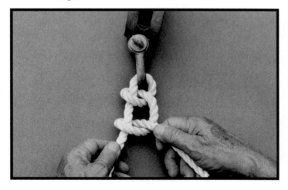

3. Pull up snug.

4. For a more secure knot with less tendency to jam, precede the two Half Hitches with a Round Turn.

Reef Knot

The well-known, widely used square knot

To Tie...

1. With first end in RH, cross it over and around second end in LH. Now hold second end in RH and first end in LH. (This is an Overhand Knot, the first step in tying your shoelace. See Page 21.)

2. With RH, cross second end behind first.

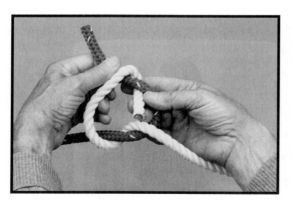

3. Then, holding second end with LH, with RH tuck first end through Bight of second end.

4. Pull snug and even. It is important to tie this well-known knot the same way each time. Tied "backwards," it becomes a Granny Knot, which is unsafe.

Use...

- A general utility knot, quickly made and easily untied.
- Joins two lines or ends of the same line when strain is not great.
- Widely used on sail gaskets (usually slipped), reef points, and lashings.

To Untie...

1. Hold Standing Part of one line in LH and the end of the same line in RH.

2. Jerk hands sharply apart to straighten line. Other line now forms two reversed Half Hitches.

3. Slip other line.

Note: The Reef Knot is never used for running rigging. Under strain, it may capsize into two reversed Half Hitches and come untied.

Clove Hitch (CROSSING KNOT)

A simple, light-duty, short-term hitch

To Tie...

1. With RH, pass eight-inch end over and around Fixed Object, coming up to the right of the Standing Part. Hold Standing Part with LH.

2. With RH, lead end toward the left over both Standing Part and Fixed Object. Hold crossing between left thumb and forefinger.

5. Work knot snug.

Use...

- As a Crossing Knot, this hitch holds a line secure to a series of Fixed Objects such as stanchions.
- Forms a temporary lifeline on deck for seagoing boats.
- Also used for roping off an area.

3. With RH, make another turn around Fixed Object to the left of the first turn.

4. With RH, reach down between second turn and Fixed Object, and pull end back up.

Clove Hitch (TEMPORARY HITCH)

A quickly tied, indispensable hitch

To Tie...

1. Take Standing Part in LH at point where Hitch is to be made. About two feet (60 cm) toward the end, grasp line with RH to make a two-foot Open Bight.

2. With LH, cast this Bight over the Fixed Object by bringing the Standing Part over the Fixed Object to the right, with the Bight catching the Fixed Object. LH crosses over RH.

5. With LH on Standing Part, and RH on End, pull snug.

Use...

- A quick, temporary way to secure a line to a bitt, bollard, and so forth.
- A fast restraint for bundling sails to spars.

3. With RH, pick up end to the right of Standing Part and make another Open Bight as in Step 1, Page 30.

4. Again with LH, cast this Bight over Fixed Object exactly as in Step 2, Page 30.

Rolling Hitch

An important, easily adjusted hitch

To Tie...

1. With Standing Part leading from right, hold end in LH. With RH, take two Turns with end to the right, that is, back in direction from which the strain on the line will come. Some sailors want the second Turn to overlap the first. We have not found any advantage, or disadvantage, to this method. Practice tying Hitches with strain in either direction.

2. With RH, cross end over Standing Part to the left.

5. When applying strain, depending on sizes and types of rope, it may be necessary to hold and twist the Hitch with one hand until the tension twists the Fixed Object to obtain the Nip. A great convenience of the Rolling Hitch is that when the strain is released, the knot can be moved in either direction.

Use...

- Bending one line to another, taut line, as when relieving the load on a genoa sheet to remove an overriding turn.
- Forms a loop that is easily adjustable when strain is released.
- Used to secure and adjust the length of the mizzen staysail tack pendant.
- Makes a handy preventer.

3. Continuing with RH, and in the same direction as other turns, take a Turn over Fixed Object and tuck the end back up through the Bight—this is similar to a Clove Hitch, but has an extra Turn.

4. Pull snug. Slide knot along Fixed Object to desired position to take strain on Fixed Object. Then pull as snug as possible.

Becket Hitch

A sheet bend used as a hitch

To Tie...

1. With LH, hold eye splice pointing toward you. With RH, tuck an eight-inch (20-cm) end of line up through the eye splice.

2. Continuing with RH through eye, with LH reach behind eye to the right and pull end to the left around back of splice.

5. When the line is much smaller than the eye splice it's being hitched to, an extra Round Turn may be added with the tying line for more security.

6. It is then a Double Becket Hitch.

Use...

- Bending a heaving line to a Monkey Fist
- Bending a line to any eye splice or loop in a line
- Although the Becket Hitch is sometimes called the Becket Bend and is basically the same knot as the Sheet Bend, it is properly a Hitch.

3. Still with LH, tuck end between Standing Part and both sides of eye splice.

4. Pull up snug.

Starting Technique

Learn this trick of the trade

Here's a special way to start tying some knots, hitches, and bends that appear on the following pages—the Sheet Bend, Bowline (Fixed Loop), Bowline (Fixed Object), Carrick Bend, and part of the Lashing Hitch.

It's an important technique to learn because it makes tying these knots easier and faster than most other methods. Apart from the Lashing Hitch, these knots all begin with the same basic motion which quickly places one line in the Closed Bight of another line.

1.

2.

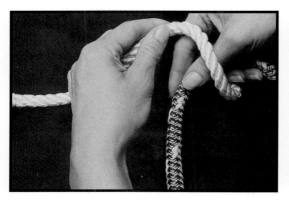

5.

6.

This motion isn't easy to describe, so these pictures show it in more detail than we will show for each separate knot's "To Tie" description. Once you "see" it, we are certain you will have no difficulty mastering it.

Perform the motion mostly with your right hand, and hold the left hand relaxed.

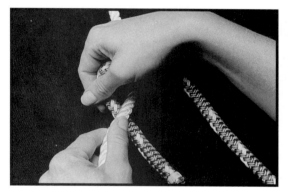

3.

4.

7.

8.

Sheet Bend

The basic, no-frills bend

To Tie...

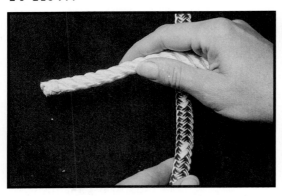

1. Remembering the Starting Technique outlined on Pages 36 and 37, with LH, hold the end of the first line (pointing toward you). With the RH, bring an eight-inch (20-cm) end of the second line (pointing away from you) down on Standing Part of the first line beyond the LH. (The fingers of the RH should be just over the Standing Part and resting on the first line.)

2. With the palm of the RH facing down, with one continuous motion rotate the right wrist, down and around the Standing Part of the first line.

5. With LH, reach under Standing Part of the first line, pull end of second line back under Standing Part, and return end to thumb and forefinger of RH, passing it over the cross of the Bight.

Use...

- Excellent for joining two lines of roughly the same diameter.
- A quick way to form a bend for light loads, but not good for maximum loads.
- A Double Sheet Bend joins slippery synthetic lines and lines of dissimilar size.

3. This forms a Closed Bight in the first line with the second line through it.

4. Finish with the second line to the right of the first line.

6. Move LH to hold Standing Part of first line, and with end and Standing Part of second line in RH, pull snug. As with the Becket Hitch, Page 35, the Sheet Bend should be doubled for use with slippery synthetics or lines of dissimilar size.

Bowline (FIXED LOOP)

The king of knots—a "must" for all

To Tie...

1. Hold Standing part in LH, with an eight-inch (20-cm) end in RH, with the open Bight near you. This Bight will form a fixed loop when the knot is tied. Always start to tie this Bowline from this position. Then you will not become confused when tying the Bowline around a Fixed Object (Page 42).

2. Remembering the Starting Technique (Page 36), with RH bring end (pointing away from you) down on Standing Part beyond LH. The fingers of your RH should be just over the Standing Part.

5. With LH, reach under Standing Part, pull the end back under the Standing Part, and return to RH, passing it over the cross of the Bight.

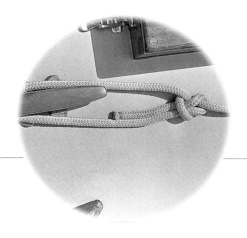

Use...

- The Bowline (pronounced BOE-lin) is the best knot to form a non-slip loop in the end of a line. It can be tied quickly, it is very secure, and it will not jam.
- Used to join sheets to headsails.
- Not easily shaken undone by flapping sails.
- Makes a fixed loop to drop over a mooring cleat or bollard.

3. With the palm of your RH facing down, in one continuous motion rotate your right wrist—down, around the Standing Part, back toward you, up, and forward again—finishing with the palm up.

4. This forms a closed Bight in the Standing Part with the fingers of RH in the Bight (palm up), and with the end through the closed Bight to the right of the Standing Part.

6. Move LH to hold the Standing Part, and with the end and the right part of the fixed loop in RH, pull snug. Note that the Bowline around a Fixed Object, Page 42, is tied differently from this Bowline. There the end is brought up under the Standing Part. Here the end is brought down.

Bowline (AROUND FIXED OBJECT)

A second bowline for different applications

To Tie...

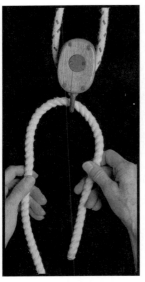

1. Remembering the Starting Technique (Page 36), but with upward motion instead of down, pass a one-foot (30-cm) end through or around the Fixed Object with LH. Always pass line from left to right. Hold Standing Part in LH near Fixed Object. Hold eight-inch (20-cm) end, pointing toward you, in RH.

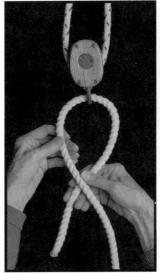

2. With RH, bring end up, under Standing Part, and between your body and LH. (The fingers of RH should be just under Standing Part.)

5. With LH, reach over the Standing Part and pull end back to the left over the Standing Part. Return it to RH underneath the cross of the Bight.

6. With the Standing Part in LH, and with the end in RH, pull snug. Note that the end is inside the Bight. If tied incorrectly, with the end outside the Bight, the Bowline can loosen or become untied when it is dragged by a shroud or stay.

Use...

- Used to pass around or through an object—for example, another bight or ring.
- Joining two lines of different sizes—Bowline through Bowline.
- Quick to tie, secure in use, and will not jam.

3. Keep end in RH and rotate, in one continuous motion with right wrist up, away from you, down through the loop and back toward you.

4. The end is now to the right of Standing Part, pointing down through the loop.

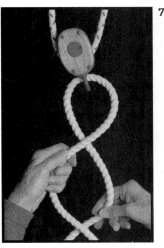

7. Note: If, after Step 1, you find that you have the end in your LH by mistake, transfer the end to the RH under the Standing Part. Proceed with Step 2, even though the end and the Standing Part are crossed. The knot will turn over when strain is applied. Note also that the Fixed Loop Bowline (Page 40) is tied differently from this Bowline. There the end is brought down over the Standing Part. Here the end is brought up under the Standing Part

Carrick Bend

A decorative but very useful knot

To Tie...

1. Remembering the Starting Technique, with LH hold end of first line pointing toward you. With RH, bring a 12-inch (30-cm) end of the second line (pointing away from you) down on the Standing Part of the first line, beyond the LH. The fingers of the RH should be just over the Standing Part.

2. With the palm of the RH facing down, in one continuous motion rotate the wrist down and around the Standing Part of the first line.

5. Continue with the RH under the LH and under the end of the second line and over the Closed Bight of the first line.

6. Let go of the second line with the RH. With the RH, reach up through the Closed Bight and pull the end of the second line back down through the Bight. The end must pass over the Standing Part of the second line where it crosses the Bight.

Use...

- The best knot for bending together two lines of the same size, or nearly the same size, quickly and securely. Faster than two Bowlines.
- This knot forms the basis for the Turk's Head, which is used to decorate a line, stanchion, or the king spoke of a wheel.

3. Finish the motion by bending the wrist up and forward again, so that the palm faces up. This forms a closed bight in the first line with second line up through it and to the right of the first line.

4. Hold the Bight of the first line and the end of the second line under the left thumb and forefinger. Move the RH down the Standing Part of second line about six inches (15 cm) and then bring the Standing Part clockwise over the end of the first line.

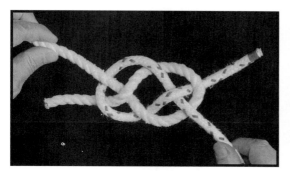

7. The Carrick Bend in its decorative form. In sailing-ship days, when used to bend two hawsers together, the ends were seized to the Standing Parts and the knot did not capsize.

8. Hold the Standing Part of the first line in your LH and the Standing Part of the second line in your RH. Jerk your hands sharply apart to capsize the knot into its modern working form.

Bowline in a Bight

A superior way to form a mid-line loop

To Tie...

1. Get two or three feet (60 cm to 1 m) of slack in the Bight of the line. With the LH, hold the line where you want a Bowline. With the RH, moving clockwise, make a small Closed Bight. Hold the crossing with the thumb and forefinger of your LH.

2. Move the RH down the line and continue clockwise to make a larger, second Closed Bight over the first—this forms the fixed loop. Lay the second Bight on top of the cross of the small first Bight.

5. With the RH, pull the fixed loop back up through the first Bight. Shift the LH to the Standing Part to release the Bights.

Use...

- A method of making a fixed loop in the middle of a long line where the ends are not accessible. Another line can then be bent to the loop, as here with a Double Becket Hitch. Also handy for making a bridle, as when hoisting a dinghy.
- Several, at intervals along a towline, can be used to tow a fleet of dinghies.

3. Again, move the RH down the line and continue clockwise to make a Turn around the small first Bight (but not around the fixed loop). Hold the cross of this turn, together with the other two crosses, with the thumb and forefinger of your LH.

4. Let go the Standing Part with the RH. With the RH, tuck the fixed loop (second Bight) up through the small first Bight.

6. Adjust the loop to the size required. Pull knot snug.

Draw Hitch

A fast, easy-to-tie, temporary hitch

To Tie...

1. This Hitch is formed from three Open Bights. Make the first Open Bight with the end on the right of the Standing Part. With your RH, pass the Bight under or through the Fixed Object.

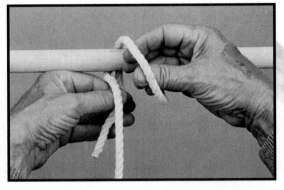

2. Pull the Bight down around the Fixed Object to the Standing Part with the RH.

5. Holding the third Bight in your RH, pull the Standing Part with your LH to tighten. Work the knot snug. This third Bight is the toggle that holds the knot together.

   To untie, pull the end smartly. A painter end can be long enough to be led back to dinghy, where it can be pulled to release this Hitch.

Use...

- Securing a halyard temporarily to a lifeline.
- Making a dinghy painter fast to a pier rail.
- Holding a bucket lanyard temporarily to a rail.
- This hitch is very quickly untied, but is insecure, and should not be used for heavy loads or long periods.

3. Make a small second Bight in the Standing Part by reaching through the first Bight with the RH to pick up the Standing Part and pull it back through the first Bight. Continue to hold with your RH.

4. Make a third open Bight in the end with the LH, and tuck the end through the second Bight to your RH.

Constrictor

A knot that binds tightly and holds fast

To Tie...

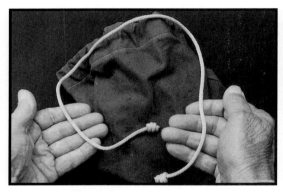

1. Hold line in both hands about twelve inches (30 cm) apart, making an Open Bight away from you.

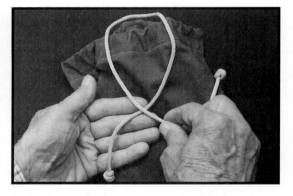

2. With your RH, twist (flip) the right part over the left part to form a Closed Bight. Hold the crossing with your left thumb and forefinger.

5. With your LH, fold the farthest Bight down, forward, and under the other parts of the knot.

6. Match the two Bights.

Use...

- An unusual knot with dozens of applications, including temporary whipping, lashing, and closing the mouth of a ditty bag.
- An excellent knot for binding.
- Draws up quickly and will not back off.

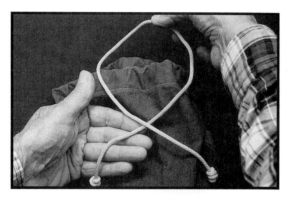

3. With your right thumb and forefinger, pick up the center of the Bight and twist it so that the right side of the Bight moves toward you.

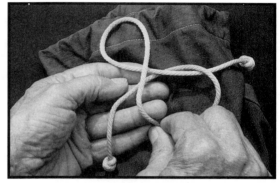

4. Still with the RH, continue to pull the Bight toward you while twisting clockwise to place the center of the Bight on top of the crossing. The Bight now forms two small Closed Bights which look like a figure eight.

7. Place the Bights over the Fixed Object (Ditty Bag). Pull the ends as snug as use of the knot requires.

8. This knot is so tenacious, it sometimes must be cut free, unless it is slipped. If quick release is desired, the knot should be slipped. After Step 4, with your RH make a small Open Bight in the right end. Then bring the right end back to the left, under the crossing. This makes a third Bight, which is the slip knot. Proceed with Steps 5 and 6 on this page. Then pull the left end and the third Bight to make the knot snug.

Lashing Hitch

This unusual knot pulls loads down tight

To Tie...

1. With a line secured aloft, pass the end through a Fixed Object on deck. With your LH, hold the end three feet (1 m) from the Fixed Object. With your RH, reach under the end to grasp the Standing Part.

2. With your RH, pull a Bight in the Standing Part back toward you and to the left, past your LH.

5. The LH now holds the two Bights, while the RH pulls the end tight to snug up knot and pull slack out of all parts, as well as to make the Standing Part of the line as taut as required.

6. With the thumb and forefinger, the LH holds the crossing of the end through the loop made by the first Bight, while the RH makes a small bight in the end about six inches (15 cm) to the right of the LH.

Use...

- A quick method of securing the dinghy on deck, gear, or sails.
- Used anywhere a load needs to be pulled down tight.
- Secures a lazy halyard where a cleat is not available and the halyard must not foul other lines.

3. With the RH still holding the Bight and the LH holding the end, use your RH to take the Bight down over the Standing Part about twelve inches (30 cm) from where the parts cross.

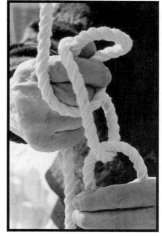

4. Continue down, around and up, using the Starting Technique described on Page 36, and place the Bight in the RH in a small Closed Bight in the Standing Part about twelve inches (30 cm) above where the end crosses the Standing Part. Drop the end in the LH, and with the LH help the RH finish forming the Bight in the Standing Part.

7. With the RH, make a Slipped Half Hitch with the Bight in the end.

8. Snug the Slipped Half Hitch back against the Bight in the Standing Part. (This makes it easy to untie, but add another Slipped Half Hitch if the knot needs to be secure.) To clear the deck, the remaining part of the end may be made up in a Gasket Coil.

Towboat Hitch

A working hitch that earns its keep

To Tie...

1. Facing the winch with the Standing Part leading behind you, take a clockwise Turn (not a Round Turn) with a long end around the winch.

2. With your LH, reach under the Standing Part to pull a three-foot (1-meter) Bight in the end under the Standing Part. Allow rope to slip through the RH.

5. With the LH, pull a third Bight under the Standing Part to the left, and place over the winch.

Use...

- Quickly secures heavy hawsers to bollards or bitts on ships, towboats (tugboats), and piers. The hitch is positive but can be easily cast off as the nip comes from the number of Turns.
- On yachts, it may be hitched over a winch when a cleat is not available. Good with wet, stiff, large ropes.

3. Without twisting, lift this bight up with the LH, over and down on the winch. Pull snug.

4. With the RH, pull a second Bight under the Standing Part to the right, and place over the winch. Pull snug.

6. If the hitch is to be left unattended, make a Slipped Half Hitch around the Standing Part with the end. Cast off by lifting each Bight from the top of the winch.

    The last turn may be held for control if tension is still required.

Eye Splice (THREE-STRANDED)

Forms a permanent eye in a rope end

All types of rope—natural fiber, synthetic fiber, and wire—can be spliced. Eye splices are useful because they share a load so evenly among their strands that they reduce the strength of the line by only 5 percent or so. By comparison, a Bowline, substituting for an Eye Splice, will weaken a rope by 45 percent. Even ordinary Hitches reduce the strength by more than 30 percent.

Wire rope is difficult to splice because its strands are stiff and inflexible. A wire-to-rope splice is easier than wire-to-wire, but it is difficult to gauge the correct tension between the two different materials without a good deal of experience.

A splice in braid is a fairly complex matter. All rope manufacturers publish detailed brochures on how to splice their braided ropes, but a different-size fid is required for each size rope. All types of braid require their own method of splicing, so most sailors let the boatyard rigger splice braid. Splicing used braid is more difficult since it is hard to insert one part into another as the rope gets stiffer with age.

That leaves stranded lines, but there are at least fifty types of splices in stranded rope. We have limited ourselves to a description of the simplest and most often used splice, the Eye Splice in Stranded Rope. (See also Cutting Rope, Page 85.)

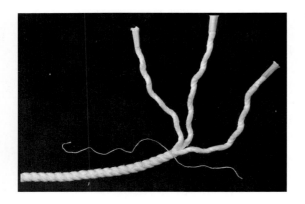

1. **From the end, at a point nine times the rope's diameter, clap on a Constrictor Knot (Page 50), using sail twine. Unlay the three strands back to the seizing, and place a small piece of tape on each end. Spread out the strands.**

Use...

- Forms an eye to drop over a mooring post, bollard, Samson post, or cleat.
- When the Standing Part is pulled through the eye, it forms an instant sliding noose—a loop of any size needed.
- When the opposite end of the line is taken through a mooring ring and passed back through the eye, it forms a permanent, unshakable hitch.

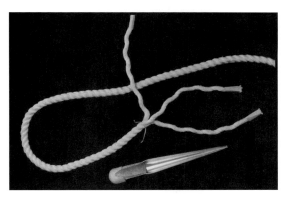

2. Make an eye in the rope of the size required and untwist the rope half a turn so the eye will not be twisted when done.

3. With an open fid, open a strand in the Standing Part at the point where the "crotch" of the splice will be. Tuck the center strand through the opening. As each strand is tucked, untwist it slightly so it lies flat in the tuck.

(continued)

Eye Splice (THREE-STRANDED)...CONTINUED

4. In the rope strand immediately to the left in the Standing Part, open another Bight. Tuck the second strand through that Bight. Turn the work toward you and open a Bight in the remaining rope strand. Tuck the third strand.

5. Pull each strand up snug, not tight, checking that the three strands are in the same tier of Bights in the rope.

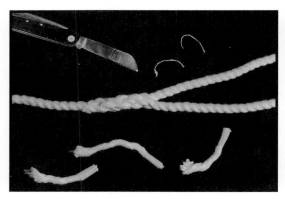

8. Cut off the end of each strand about a quarter-inch (6 mm) from the rope. Melt each end with a match or a hot knife so the strands will not unlay. Carefully cut the Constrictor.

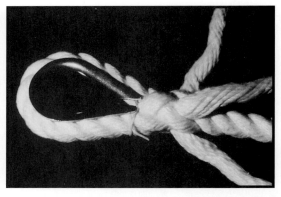

9. An Eye Splice around a thimble (usually galvanized steel) in either braided or stranded rope protects the rope from wear in heavy-duty uses, such as receiving a shackle that connects the anchor rode to the anchor chain.

Tools Used...

- Clockwise from top: Open or Swedish fid, spool of sail twine, rigger's knife with becket for a lanyard, marlinspike.

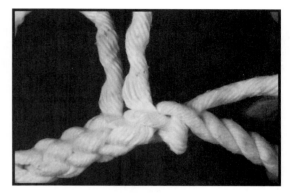

6. Lead each strand over the adjacent one and tuck it through the Bight in the next strand. Pull the strands tight. Repeat these steps for two more tiers. Each strand now has been tucked three times.

7. To taper the splice, select one strand and tuck once. Select the next strand and tuck it twice, The three strands are now strung out along the rope, forming a taper.

Again, please remember there are more than fifty splices for stranded rope. Some sailors tuck four full tucks, and a few tuck six. Some taper by cutting out one-half the strand, and some by cutting out one-third before the final two or three tucks. Experience will teach you what best suits each application.

One variation on the Eye Splice is the Anchor Splice, where the line is passed through the last link in the anchor chain without a thimble, then spliced into the Standing Part. Done right, each strand bears fairly on the link, prevents movement, and minimizes chafe. The diameter of the splice is also kept as small as the chain's, so that the splice can pass through the deck pipe to the chain locker, and this is its big advantage over the alternative of a thimbled Eyesplice shackled to the chain.

All About Coils

Proper coiling means safety

Untangling Fouled Lines

1. When a line is lying in a tangled heap it must be cleared as soon as possible. Loosen as much as you can shaking gently.

2. Then, without forcing, roll the Standing Part up and out from the center of the tangle and continue to loosen by shaking the fouled parts. Coil the cleared part neatly alongside.

The Importance of Coiling

What you do with rope when it's not being used is very important. Lines must be carefully coiled and well secured so that they run free when needed. A fouled coil is dangerous to ship and crew.

In general, sheets should be made fast with a Cleat Coil, especially if the boat is heeling and/or taking seas aboard, which would deliver the coil to the cockpit sole in a tangled mess. However, some sailors drop the loose coil over the winch and coils may not have to be made fast if it is not too rough or the boat is small so that the sheet is short. There may be objection to this, but a wet, loose sheet sloshing around the sole is dangerous and probably will become fouled.

How to Make Safe Coils

A quick and secure method

1. With the line to be coiled leading away from you, hold the end in your LH. This end should be three feet (1 meter) long for a Gasket or Stowage Coil. The Standing Part leading to the cleat should be eight inches (20 cm) long for a Cleat Coil.

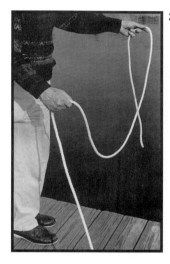

2. Take the Standing Part loosely in the RH with an Open Bight between the hands. Extend both arms fully, letting the line slide through your RH to make the first Bight.

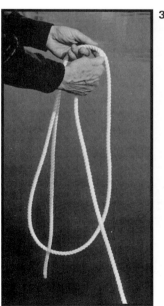

3. Lower your arms, bringing the RH to the LH and twisting the line clockwise with your right thumb and forefinger to remove twist from the Bight. Take each Bight in the LH. Repeat Steps 2 and 3 until all the line is coiled.

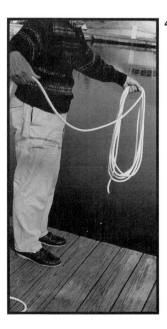

4. Make each Bight the same size, twisting each enough to make it lie fair. If the Bights will not lie fair, with each Bight kinking more than the last, don't fight it. Uncoil, and work out the twists in the line along the deck. A line that is too long or too big to hold in one hand should be coiled on deck.

Common Coil

Quickest way to secure a coil

To Tie...

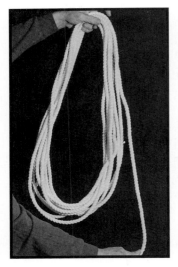

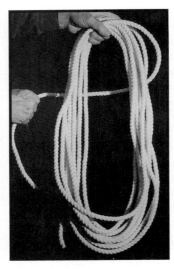

1. Make up the coil leaving a four-foot (1.2 m) end. Hold coil in your LH, and with your RH hold the end about eighteen inches (45 cm) from the coil.

2. With the RH, take a counterclockwise Round Turn down under the coil around the back to the front, ending up in front.

3. Still holding the coil in the LH, with the RH pass a short Bight through coil from front to back. The Bight passes above the Turn at the back of the coil.

- **The Common Coil is the easiest way to secure a coil when both ends are free.**
- **Holds unused line clear of the decks to avoid fouling.**
- **Quickly undone to free line for use without kinks.**

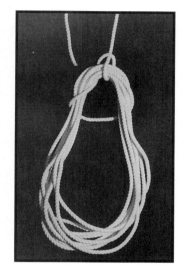

4. **Hold the Bight with the LH, and with the RH tuck the end up, over the coil, and through the Bight.**

5. **The completed coil.**

Casting Off a Coil

After inspecting that the bights are fair, lay the coil on the deck with the end underneath. Again, inspect for bights that obviously won't run out. If the coil is large or looks suspicious, lift it up and pay it out by starting with the end. Place it to one side and then drop each Bight on the deck near the end until all the line is in a heap. Make sure that none of the Bights are on top of the end. Do this deliberately—it will save time.

Cleat Coil

A seamanlike way to hitch a coil to a cleat

To Tie...

1. Hold the top of the coil in your LH with about eight inches (20 cm) of the Standing Part between the coil and the cleat.

2. With your RH, reach through the coil and pull the Standing Part back through it to form a small open Bight.

5. . . . then rehook.

Uses...

- The hitch most often used to secure a coiled halyard fall to its cleat.
- Prevents tangling and kinking that could cause serious trouble.
- Holds halyard ready for instant release.

3. With your RH, hook the Bight over the top horn of the cleat.

4. If the coil is not snug against the cleat because the Bight is too long, unhook the Bight and with RH twist it counterclockwise to shorten it . . .

Gasket Coil

A more permanent way to stow a coil

To Tie...

1. Start the coil with the end that does not have a shackle or an eye splice. The shackle or splice may then conveniently be looped over a hook in the gear locker. When ready for use, the shackle (the business end) is again available on top of the coil. Coil the line until a four-foot (1.2-m) end remains.

2. With your RH, make three or four Turns tightly around the coil with the end, about six inches (15 cm) below the top. Work down the coil. Continue Turns until about two feet (60 cm) of the end is left.

3. With your RH, make a one-foot (30-cm) Bight in the end. Tuck it through the eye of the coil above the Round Turns.

Uses...

- A good coil for stowing a jib or spinnaker sheet that has a snap shackle in one end.
- Simple to tie, and very secure, this method is useful where there is no cleat or belaying pin to hang the coil on.

4. With your RH, pull the Bight back over the top of the coil.

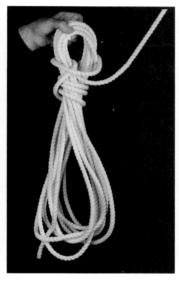

5. Pull down against Turns.

6. Pull the end to remove any slack and work all the parts snug. To untie, pull the Bight back over the top of the coil.

Stowage Coil

Neat, shipshape stowage

To Tie...

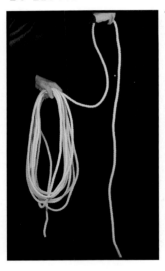

1. Hold the coil in your LH.

2. With your RH, make an Open Bight two feet (60 cm) long in the end by lifting the RH until the end can be grasped by the left thumb.

5. Drop the Bight behind the coil, again over your left forefinger, and with your RH reach through the coil and pull the Bight back through.

6. Again, use your forefinger to keep an opening. With your RH, tuck the Bight from left to right under the previous Bight, to the left of the first tuck.

Uses...

- An excellent way to maintain a secure coil when the line is stowed with other gear.
- It takes time to make up, but it keeps the bights fair in the coil.
- A Bristol-fashion way to finish a mainsheet coil.

3. Drop this Bight behind the coil and over your left forefinger. With your RH, reach through the coil and pull the Bight back through.

4. With your RH, tuck the Bight from right to left under the Standing Part of the Bight on top of the coil. Lift your left forefinger to make way for the tuck.

7. Pull snug. Fair up all Turns. Then pull tight.

Utility Line Stowage

A special method of coiling stiff lines

Uses...

• A boat's shore utility lines—for water, electricity, TV, and telephone service—are stiff and inflexible.

• This special coiling procedure obviates the half-turn introduced into each Bight by conventional coiling.

• Leaves gear ready to be handled, free of twists.

To Tie...

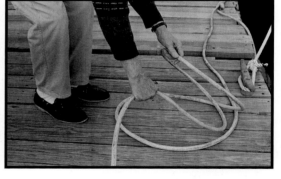

1. With RH, lay down one clockwise turn on the pier or deck. With LH, hold Standing Part near Turn.

2. With RH, lead Standing Part down and out to the right, then up and back under LH to put in the second Turn. The Standing Part is now under this Turn.

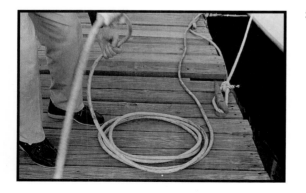

3. Fair the Turn and put it down over the first Turn. Repeat Steps 1 through 3 until slack is taken up, and the coil is completed. Finally, seize Turns with a Slipped Reef Knot, using light cordage.

Modern Deck Hardware

Fast for racers, convenient for cruisers

Pages 22 and 23 show the preferred belay to a traditional horned cleat. Today, however, cam cleats have replaced horned cleats for the mainsheet on many boats, and some halyard cleats are being replaced with rope clutches. Coupled with deck organizers, rope clutches enable one winch to handle as many lines as can be fairly led to the winch drum. A deck organizer is a group of deck-mounted cheek blocks that act as fairleads from the turning blocks at the base of the mast to the rope clutches fronting the halyard winch. An organizer may also be installed between the clutches and the winch.

When engaged, most rope clutches allow lines to be heaved in, but not paid out. To disengage the clutch, raise the lever on top of the clutch body. When releasing a loaded clutch, ensure sufficient turns on the drum to hold the line. If the clutch won't release, take up on the winch to unload the clutch. (Many clutches now allow controlled release of a fully loaded line.)

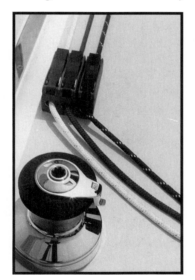
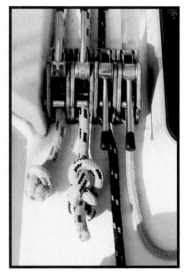

(Courtesy Harken)

Left: Sheets and controls distributed over turning blocks to cam cleats on a modern racing sailboat. Many cruising sailboats use a cam cleat only for the mainsheet, if at all. Top left: A deck organizer redirects halyards on their way from the mast base to a cockpit-mounted winch. Top center and right: Two varieties of rope clutches, one showing another use for stopper knots.

Winches

Sophisticated devices to make life easier afloat

Winches, regardless of whether they're mounted to port or to starboard, are designed to take clockwise turns (wraps) of line. There are specialized winches for various uses aboard different types of sailing craft, including snubbing, top or bottom action, single or variable speed, pedestal operated, power (hydraulic or electric) driven, and manual winches.

Most contemporary winches are self-tailing, so they can be operated by a single crew member. The winch drum is fitted with a spring-operated track, which acts as a jam-cleat around its circumference at the top, and a protruding "stripping arm." The final wrap on the drum is placed in the track, and as the winch is operated, the line is "tailed," or held, by the track and then pulled out of the track by the stripping arm. Coupled with a series of rope clutches or cleats, one self-tailing winch mounted on the cabin top enables a single crew member to manage many sail controls—halyards, lifts, reefing lines, and more.

A ratchet is built into the single-speed winch (either in the mechanism itself or in the handle) so that the handle can be positioned to afford the crew member the best possible leverage against the loaded line. This feature is invaluable when trying to "sweat-in" the last few inches on a taut halyard or sheet.

Of multiple-speed winches, the two-speed is the most

Self-tailing winches save labor when the wind kicks up.

common. They have two gears, high and low. These gears can be engaged as needed by turning the winch handle either counter-clockwise or clockwise. High gear is designed to retrieve the line quickly. As the line becomes taut with load, the direction of handle rotation can be switched to shift into low gear for the final "sweating-in." Low gear changes the gear ratio

A self-tailing winch; the stripper arm on top of the drum is pointing at the viewer.

so that more power, usually three or four times more, is applied to the load. There is a proportional loss of speed when using low gear, as compared with high gear, but when the two are used one after the other, sheets and halyards can be pulled in or up tighter and faster.

Top-action drum winches and the most common self-tailing winches have removable handles that mount on top of the drum. A spring-loaded lock prevents the handle from popping out of the drum and maybe going over the side. Even though fiber and plastic handles float, retrieving them is rarely easy. Make sure the lock works freely and that the handle is always fully inserted into the winch. A handle is very dangerous when it slips, since the arm flies in a wide circle.

Nonetheless, since there are still in service thousands of the non-self-tailing winches that require teamwork, we describe their operation on Page 74.

(Courtesy Harken)

Overriding Turns

What to do when it happens

Since the drum of a winch will not turn counter-clockwise, line can be paid out only if the Turns are slack. When either the Standing Part or the end is allowed to cross over a Turn or Turns, there is an override, and the line will not feed off the drum because of the friction holding the Turns.

1. The overriding Turn nips the Turn or Turns under it by crossing over them.

   If the override is allowed to go too far, the line cannot be heaved in or paid out because the Standing Part across the top Turn prevents the line from leaving the winch. The winch is useless and the line cannot be moved either way. In an emergency the line

is cut to free it. Overrides occur when the lead is poor, either too high for the Standing Part leading to the winch, or too low for the end being slacked off. Too much slack in line approaching or leaving the winch also may cause an override.

2. Watch for an overriding Turn. As soon as one starts, heave in or pay out until it clears. Often a jam can be cleared by leading the end counter-clockwise back around the drum and then to another winch. Strain from the second winch pulls the Bight out from under the overriding Turn. If the Standing Part is still under great tension, set up a Preventer before clearing the winch. See next paragraph.

3. When the Standing Part jams so badly it can't be cleared, bend another sheet to the clew, if it can be reached. If not, bend a line to the Standing Part of the fouled line with a Rolling Hitch. Lead this relieving line to another winch to take the strain off the Standing Part. Then the jam can easily be cleared. Note: Never touch any part of the line on the winch until the preventer is rigged and holding.

Sheet Winches—HAULING IN

Safe usage requires care

The Method...

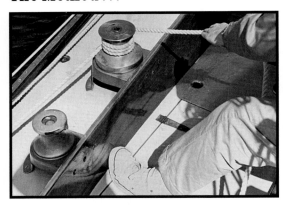

1. Two crew usually are detailed to operate a non self-tailing sheet winch, one to tail the sheet and another to crank the handle. The tailer decides which cleat will be used and if other lines will be in the way.

    The tailer puts as many turns on the drum as are needed to hold the load of the sail when partially trimmed. Don't expect to take turns on the winch as the sail is filling—if a sudden puff of wind comes, the sail will take charge. The lead of the sheet must be clear. When the clew of the jib is clear of the lee shrouds in coming about, the tailer takes a strain on the sheet by hauling the line hand-over-hand as fast as possible, maintaining tension on the sheet at all times. If slack gets in the line for any reason, the inertia of the spinning drum easily causes an override.

4. When the handle can no longer be turned freely, the cranker sweats in the last few inches by pushing the handle away, using the ratchet to bring the handle back for another purchase.

Safety Tips...

- If you're tailing, don't let your hands get closer than eight inches (20 cm) to the winch. A spinning handle could slash your knuckles. If the line slips, your fingers could get caught in the turns.
- Make sure the handle is locked in place. If it flies out, you could lose it overboard. Worse, it could strike and hurt the tailer or another crewmember.
- Don't stand in the bight of a loaded turning block. If the block were to let go, you could be seriously injured.

2. When the slack is in, the tailer snaps on one or two more Turns so that the line will not slip on the winch drum. The tailer must keep his or her hands clear of the winch, guide the line low enough to clear the handle, and pull hard enough to keep the line from slipping.

3. After the last turn goes on, the cranker fits the handle as the drum stops turning. With the feet placed to give good balance and power, the cranker turns the handle 360 degrees with both hands.

The Finishing Touches

After the sheet has been properly trimmed, the tailer should belay the sheet, but not make it fast until he receives that order. The handle may now be unshipped and stowed in its pocket, or wherever the skipper directs. Finally, the tailer clears the end of the sheet from other lines and sees that it is free to run when needed.

Meanwhile, the cranker clears the weather sheet, taking two or three Turns on the winch, setting things up for the next tack. Slack should be taken out of the weather sheet to make sure it's not trailing overboard in the water, but no strain should be put on it.

Halyard Drum Winches —HOISTING

Taking the strain out of raising sail

To Hoist...

1. Select a cleat with a good lead from the winch. Make sure the halyard is clear aloft—check the headstay for halyard wraps. Does the end have a Stopper Knot to stop it disappearing into the mast aloft? Cast on two or three clockwise Turns.

2. When the command to hoist is given, heave in quickly hand-over-hand until the halyard is taut.

3. Cast on one or two more Turns depending on the size of the sail. Hold halyard in your LH inboard, and install the winch handle with your RH outboard.

4. Crank and tail until the luff is very taut.

5. Make the halyard fast on the cleat and secure with a single Half Hitch. Remove the handle and stow it.

6. Coil the halyard carefully and secure it on the cleat.

Sheet Winch —PAYING OUT

There's as much to easing out as to hauling in

To Ease...

1. At the command "Stand by to come about," make sure the end of sheet is still clear and that you are not standing on it or in any of its Bights. Don't ever get caught in the Bight of a line.

2. Cast the figure-of-eight turns off the cleat, but keep a strain on the Round Turn still on the cleat so that not a fraction of an inch of sheet pays out. The skipper may change plans and sail another hour on this tack.

3. At command "Helm's Alee," cast off the Round Turn from cleat. When the jib "breaks" and the sheet begins to slacken, quickly free the sheet from the winch by pulling it straight up from the winch. Let go the sheet.

4. Watch the sheet to see that it runs free and that the shackle at the clew clears the shrouds and the mast. If it does foul, sing out: "Fouled sheet." The boat may have to be maneuvered to prevent the sail from being torn.

Tacking with Self-Tailing Winches

Tacking when using a large self-tailing winch requires more attention on the part of the crew releasing the sheet than would be required for a non-self-tailing winch. The stripping arm hinders the removal of the sheet straight off the top of the drum, and can injure fingers if they are pulled into the winch by a sheet under tension. Therefore, wraps must be taken off one at a time to make sure that the sheet can run free as the boat settles onto its new tack. It is imperative to keep your hands clear of the winch drum when it is in operation, as the stripper can catch fingers.

A spinnaker sheet led through a turning block to a self-tailing winch. Even in a moderate breeze there's a heavy load on this winch.

(Courtesy Harken)

Halyard Drum Winches—LOWERING

The correct way to douse a sail

To Lower...

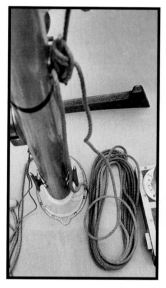

1. Capsize the coiled halyard on the deck or cabin top with the Standing Part leading from the top of the coil.

2. Cast off the halyard, keeping a strain on it so it does not slide back around the drum.

3. At the command to lower, very carefully remove one or two turns from the drum, but leave several to hold halyard from running. Take Turns off by unwinding the end all the way around the drum. Keep the end perpendicular to the drum and pulled taut to prevent all the turns from jumping off accidentally. Then ease off the halyard until luff is slack. Cast the halyard free from the winch and lower handsomely, allowing time for foredeck crew to keep sail out of the water. If the sail will fall on deck, the halyard may be let go by the run.

Picking Up a Mooring
Without yelling

For our purposes, to moor is to make a boat fast to a mooring float. Note that when she's lying to one anchor, a boat is said to be anchored, not moored. However, when two or more anchors are used, a boat is said to be moored.

At the water's surface, most permanent moorings consist of a buoy that supports the heavy mooring cable or chain, and a float that is bent by about a 10-foot (3-meter) pendant to the eye splice in the mooring cable below the buoy.

The Method...

1. The skipper will tell you from which side of the boat he wants you to pick up the mooring.
2. Fetch the boat hook.
3. Clear any lines or sails from the foredeck, the mooring cleat, and the bow chocks that may interfere with the mooring line.
4. Direct the helmsman as calmly as you can, regardless of impending disaster, toward the float. Do not aim the bow directly at float but a little to one side.

5. Hold the boathook so it is just under water and facing away from the bow.
6. As the hook approaches the float, dip the hook well down into water and swing out, catching the rope pendant next to float. As soon as pole hits the pendant, pull in.
7. If you miss, swing the pole back and try again.

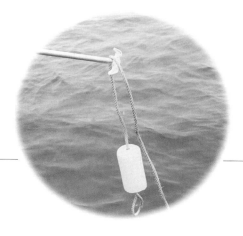

About Mooring...

- Depending on the direction of the current with reference to the wind, the skipper might need to make a practice pass before trying to pick up the float pendant.
- Never try to hang on to the pendant if it is being pulled out of your hand. You could strain your back badly. Better to let it go and make another pass.

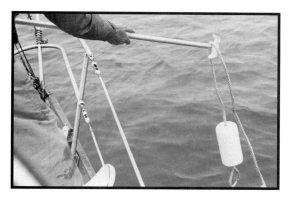

8. When hooked, pull in the pole hand-over-hand. Grasp pendant. Place the boathook on deck.

9. Lead the pendant under the lifeline to the mooring cleat. Belay until all way is stopped and the boat has fallen back, with the mooring out ahead. Then, haul in the mooring eye and drop it on the cleat.

10. With chafing gear in the chock, lash the eye splice to the cleat with the pendant by taking figure-eight turns and a Half Hitch.

Bending Flag Halyard TO FLAGSTAFF

How to send that burgee aloft

When a flagstaff is used, the flag, pennant, wind sock, or night hawk is bent permanently to the end of a staff in such a way that it can rotate 360 degrees around the staff. The halyard is bent to the flagstaff as follows:

To Tie...

1. Snap ends of halyard to each other, or bend them to each other with a Carrick Bend. A few inches above the Bend, cast a Clove Hitch on the lower end of the staff and slide the Hitch up the staff to about 12 inches (30 cm) below the flag.

2. A few inches below the Carrick Bend, cast another Clove Hitch onto the staff about two inches (50 mm) from the end. Pull this Hitch snug.

3. Slide the first Hitch up the staff until the slack is taken out between Hitches. The top Hitch should not be closer than six inches (15 cm) to the flag.

4. [Left] Work both hitches tight, then hoist slowly.

5. [Right] Keep the staff horizontal until the flag is past the backstay. Incidentally, never roll up a flag on its staff. Stow it flat, or it will take a curl that makes it more difficult to hoist past the stays.

Heaving a Line
Done calmly and deliberately, it's easy

A heaving line is technically a braided line with a rope-covered weight (a Monkey Fist) bent to one end. On a pleasure-boat, a long docking line, or even two lines bent together, is most often used.

To Heave...

1. [Not pictured] Make one end fast to a cleat, lead the line outboard, then up and back over the lifelines. Form a large Bowline in the other end if a Monkey Fist or eye splice is not used.
2. Coil all the line into your LH, making about two-foot (60-cm) Bights.
3. Divide the coil in half, with the LH holding the Standing Part half, and the RH holding the half to be heaved. Leave about four feet (1.2 m) of slack between the coils.
4. When you estimate the line is long enough to carry all the way to its objective, open the fingers of your LH so that the Bights will pay out one by one. Using the RH coil as a weight, heave it sidearm and underhand, aiming over the head of the man receiving the line. The Bights in the RH coil should stay together until they have pulled all the line from the LH.

The Aftermath

If the line misses its target, quickly re-coil it to keep it clear of the propeller. Divide the coil and heave it again.

When the dockhand has hold of the line, ask him or her to drop the Bowline or eye splice over a cleat or pile. Then you are in charge of how much to haul in. Enthusiastic helpers ashore often haul in too short, too quickly. The skipper may wish to back down on the full scope of the line, depending on the wind, the tidal stream, and other boats.

Whipping

In the end, it counts

As in Splicing, there are several different kinds of Whipping. Since this book does not include marlinespike seamanship, we will deal only with ordinary Whipping. We use stranded rope because it is slightly more complex to whip than is braided rope.

To Whip...

1. **The end of the rope is seized or melted with a hot knife. Stick a sail needle, threaded with sail twine, through the rope where the Whipping is to begin. A sailor's palm may be required for heavy and tightly laid rope.**

2. **Carefully and strongly wind the twine around the rope with each turn parallel, and snug it. Cover the protruding end of the twine with the turns. The Whipping should be as wide as the rope's diameter. We assume a right-turning Whipping, but it may also be worked to the left.**

3. **Thrust the needle between the strands next to the last turn and carefully bring the line out in the adjacent strand, next to the same turn of twine. Pull very tight.**

Cutting Rope

The best way to cut synthetic rope is with a heated knife. First let the knife get hot, then clean the blade by wiping it on a waste rag. Be sure the blade is still really hot when you begin, and cut over a piece of scrap wood.

1. **Holding the rope with one hand, slowly press the knife down one quarter of the diameter of the rope. Lift the knife clear. Rotate the rope away from you one quarter-turn. With the knife hot, press down another quarter diameter. Lift the knife clear.**

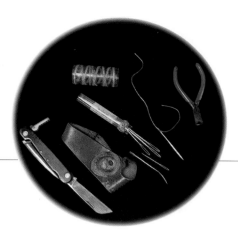

Tools Used...

- Clockwise from top: twine, nippers, needles, sailor's palm, knife.

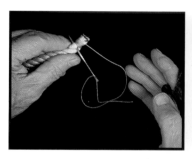

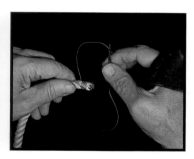

4. Cross back to the left, over the Whipping, following the groove between the two strands, to insert the needle at the first turn. This is called worming. Be certain the needle enters hard by the Whipping, and that it exits outside the turns between the farther strands. Pull very snug.

5. Cross to the right, again following the groove between two strands. Repeat Steps 3 and 4 so that all three strands are wormed. Stick the needle through the rope several times to bury the end. Cut off the twine close to the rope. The crossings may be repeated in order to worm twice, or the twine may be doubled before starting so that the whole Whipping is doubled.

6. Whip braided line the same way, except that you will have to space the worming turns without the grooves between strands for a guide.

2. Repeat twice more. The rope will be cut evenly and the edges will not be overheated.

3. With the knife at a 45-degree angle, carefully smooth the edges by turning the rope against the face of the knife.

Docking Lines

Vigilance on a falling tide

When a vessel is docked, she lies alongside a float or pier. To be over-technical, the water is the dock—hence drydock—but in common usage the pier is the dock. So the lines used to secure the boat are mostly called docking lines, although some refer to them as mooring lines. Their length depends on the length of your boat, but they usually have an eye splice in one end.

The Lineup...

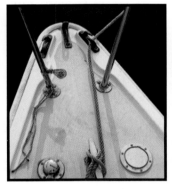

BOW LINE. It leads from the inboard bow chock ahead to the pier.

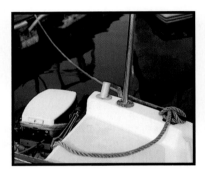

STERN LINE. It leads from the stern to the pier. The outboard chock holds the boat to the pier better than does the inboard chock.

BREAST LINES. They lead at right angles from the rail to the pier. There can be a Bow Breast, a Waist Breast, a Quarter Breast, or some combination of these. Breast lines, when led to a pier rather than a float, will go slack or taut as the water rises and falls, and must be tended regularly.

If your line must share a cleat or bollard with another line, run your line up through the Bight already in place and then drop your eye over the bollard. Either line may then be cast off without disturbing the other.

Dockline Tips...

- Docking lines should be tended from the boat, not the pier.
- If you're short-handed when leaving a berth, make one end of each docking line fast on deck. Send the other end ashore, around a bollard or cleat, then back on board to a cleat. Then you can cast these lines off and retrieve them on board with no help from ashore.

SPRING LINES. They lead fore or aft alongside the boat. The After Bow Spring or the Forward Quarter Spring should be at least as long as the boat, but a minimum of three times the height of the tide. They prevent the boat from moving ahead or astern as the tide ebbs and flows or the wind changes.

After studying where the side of the boat will bear on the pier, place fenders accordingly. Use a slipped Clove Hitch (Crossing Knot) to

secure the fender pendant to the lifeline, but reeve the end through the Bight for security.

The Yacht Tender

Securing, towing, and hoisting

The eight-foot to ten-foot (2.3-m to 3-m) fiberglass dinghy used to be the most prevalent tender for sailing yachts. Today, however, the inflatable may have superseded it, as it is easier to handle, safer, roomier, and less likely to damage the brightwork.

Securing Alongside

Most yachts have a gate in the lifelines on the starboard side. When coming alongside to deliver passengers and supplies, it is often convenient to secure the tender temporarily to the lifeline with a Draw Hitch (Page 48). If the painter is about fifteen feet (4.5 m) long, the end may be led back aboard the tender. When you're ready to shove off for the next load, you don't have to reach over the tender's bow to let go. After you're seated and ready to row, simply pull the end of the painter to capsize the Draw Hitch. If a dinghy is to be left unattended, secure the painter to a cleat or with a Bowline. Dinghies do go adrift more often than we wish.

Securing to a Mooring Pendant

To leave the tender on the mooring, the pendant is cast off the yacht with the tender's painter made fast to it. Lead the painter inboard under the bow pulpit. If the painter is short, make the end fast to the mooring pendant Bight with a Bowline. If it is long, double the painter and pass it through the Bight using the doubled line to make a Bowline.

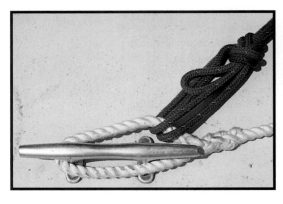

Towing Tips...

- Lighten the dinghy for towing. Remove everything you can. And remember, she'll track better if she's stern-heavy.
- Tie down everything left aboard—oars, bailer, oarlocks, and so forth—in case of capsize.
- A correctly-sized three-strand nylon painter stretches to absorb the jerks of towing better than an oversized Dacron plait.

Towing Astern—Under Power

The tender offers the least drag when towed on the forward side of the first stern wave in the wake. In this position the dinghy's bow is supported by the painter and its stern planes downhill on the forward edge of the wave. There is a minimum of wetted surface and, in good weather, no yawing.

In moderate following seas, the dinghy should be towed on the forward side of the second or third wave. If towed too closely, it may charge up, ramming the stern. In bad weather, the dinghy will be on board, lashed down.

Inflatables are often towed close astern, since if they ram the transom they do no harm. Two painters can be used, one from each side of the boat. Control is good, but the ultimate control is gained by hoisting the dinghy bow up to the taffrail. There are some who do not think this method is shipshape, however.

Towing Astern—Under Sail

Usually, a sailboat wake is not large enough to make much difference and the scope of the painter is increased to fifty feet (15 m) or more, trying to find the forward side of a wave.

Lengthening the painter cushions the dinghy's wilder jerks. The Carrick Bend should be used to add line to the painter because it can be soaked for days under strain, yanked repeatedly, and still be untied with ease.

The Yacht Tender (CONTINUED)

Hoisting Aboard

When preparing a yacht to race, strong hands can lift the dinghy aboard in seconds. Properly prepared, one person can bring the dinghy aboard quite easily using the main halyard.

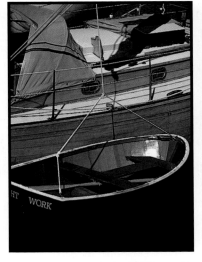

If a special bridle is not available, a sufficient one can be quickly rigged with the painter. Lead it aft from the bow of the dinghy. Above the midship thwart, cast in a Single Bowline in a Bight, leaving a small loop. Continue the painter aft through the stern ring and adjust the length with a Rolling Hitch.

If there is no stern ring, lead the painter through the port and starboard seat brackets and then put the Rolling Hitch on the Standing Part.

Secure the main halyard shackle to the Bowline. Heave in on the halyard, and fend off as the dinghy comes over the lifelines.

Place two small fenders along the inboard edge of the grab rail, then lower away until the dinghy rests between the cabin house and the lifelines. Slack the main sheet and secure the boom out of the way. Taking hold of the stern of the dinghy, capsize it onto its chocks. Secure the dinghy, using the two gripes fitted for the purpose or use a length of line criss-crossing from the bows to the opposite quarters.

Chain Hitch

Just right for dinghies

The Chain Hitch is simple, quick to tie, and very easily untied. It's fairly secure, certainly more secure than the Draw Hitch, and offers an easy method of temporarily making the dinghy fast to a ring or rail on a float or pier.

To Tie...

1. Pass small Bight in the painter under rail with LH and back over rail. Hold Bight in RH and with LH tuck a second Bight in End through first.

2. Hold with RH and pull snug.

3. Pass End in LH under Standing Part and tuck a third small Bight through the second Bight. Hold Bight with RH and pull snug.

6. To untie with LH pull End back through last Bight and jerk knot loose.

4. With LH pull End back under Standing Part and repeat Step 3.

5. With LH tuck all of End through last Bight. Do not pull snug.

Glossary of Nautical Terms

Many of the terms in this glossary have several meanings. Only the ones more pertinent to this manual are given. The page number in parentheses refers to that use of the term in the text that best illustrates it; words in italics may be found elsewhere in the glossary. A list of the 10 most common line-handling commands appears at the end of this glossary.

BACKSTAY A *stay* that keeps the *mast* from bending or leaning forward. Can be either fixed or running. Running backstays are rigged on both sides of the boat, and are set up or slacked off according to the point of sailing. (p. 82)

BATTEN A thin, narrow piece of wood or plastic inserted in a pocket in the *leech* of the sail to stiffen it.

BECKET The ring on a block or an *eye splice*.

BITT(S) A square post or pair of posts with or without a crossbar (norman) for securing heavy lines. Usually in the bow.

BOLLARD A round, heavy post for securing lines. Sometimes on a boat, but usually on a pier. (p. 87)

BOLTROPE Rope sewn in the edge of a sail.

BY THE RUN To let go a line completely without slowing the speed at which it runs out; see PAY OUT. (p. 78)

CABLE Technically, three ropes laid up left-handed. In modern practice, any large line—usually used for anchoring. Chain is also called cable. (p. 13)

CAM CLEAT See CLEAT.

CAPSIZE To turn over a coil from its stowed position so that the standing part will run free. To turn over the parts of a knot. (p. 79)

CAST IN To tie a knot or make a splice in a line.

CAST OFF To take turns off a winch or *bitt*, etc. May also imply hauling the line in after casting off, as in the case of docking lines. (p. 78)

CAST ON To put turns on a winch or *bitt*, etc. (p. 76)

CHAFING GEAR Any device of a soft material such as leather, rope, or plastic, that prevents lines, sails, decks, or *spars* from wear by rubbing. (p. 81)

CHOCK An *eye*, or partial *eye*, to hold a towing or mooring line in place where it passes through or over the rail. (p. 81)

CLEAT A fitting for belaying lines and making fast. The several types include:

CAM CLEAT A cleat in which the rope passes between two opposing, toothed, spring-loaded jaws. The jaws permit the line to be hauled in, but they grip firmly when the line tries to run back out. (p. 71)

HORNED CLEAT Traditional cleat with two opposing horns.

JAM CLEAT A horned cleat in which one horn is close to the base, forming a V-shaped groove that grips the rope. One type of jam cleat has only one horn fitted with teeth to hold the line.

CLEAT EYE A hole in the center of some *cleats* for securing the bitter end of the line in use, so that it will not come adrift. (p. 78)

CLUTCH See ROPE CLUTCH.

DAVITS Small cranes used to raise boats or anchors from water to deck level. Usually mounted in pairs for boats.

DECK ORGANIZER Fairleads with several sheaves, which serve to sort and separate halyards and other lines as they lead aft to winches, clutches, and cleats. (p. 71)

DOWNHAUL A tackle fitted to the boom gooseneck to keep a proper strain on the luff.

EYE SPLICE A closed bight (fixed loop) formed in the end of a line by splicing the end back into its standing part.

FAIR To work the parts of a knot in their proper positions. To arrange the bights in a coil so they lie in order. (p. 68)

FAIRLEAD A device such as a *block* or a *chock* to keep a line in a desired position where it will not foul other gear, or chafe.

FENDERS A round plastic tube or ball filled with air and used to cushion a boat against a pier, float or other boat. Formerly made of rope.

GASKET A short strip of sailcloth or line used to fasten a furled sail to its gaff or boom.

GILGUYS Short small lines used to hold halyards and other ropes from slatting against a mast or spar.

GUY A line, sometimes of wire, to control the position of a spar. The *spinnaker* pole has two. The after guy is usually led to a snatch block on the quarter, and the fore guy is led to a *fairlead* block at the bow.

HALYARD A line, often wire, used to hoist and lower a sail or flag.

HAND-OVER-HAND To haul in a line rapidly when it is not under strain. (p. 74)

HANDSOMELY Deliberately, carefully, with control. (p. 79)

HORNED CLEAT See CLEAT.

HORNS The two arms or projections of a horned cleat.

JACKLINE A rope rigged to the lower luff of a sail to pull it back from the mast track when reefing.

JAM CLEAT See CLEAT.

JIBE A shift of sail from one side to another with the wind astern. It can be violent if not controlled. It can be caused by a change in course (that brings the wind across the *leech* of a sail) or a by change in the direction of the wind.

LEAD (Rhymes with seed.) As a noun: The way in which a line runs between two points. It should be unobstructed. As a verb: To thread or direct, as in: "Lead the jib *sheet* outboard of the *shrouds*."

LEECH LINE A small line *rove* through the hem of the leech. It adjusts the shape of the sail and controls flutter.

LIFELINES Permanent lines rigged to keep the crew aboard in bad weather. Temporary lifelines may be set up to contain small children.

LIFT The line, rigged from a mast, that holds the outboard end of a boom or *spinnaker* pole in a desired horizontal position. Often it is called the pole *lift* or *topping lift*.

MONKEY FIST A rope knot, similar to a Turk's Head, covering a small weight. *Bent* to a *heaving line* and thrown, it has sufficient mass to pull the line behind it.

ORGANIZER See DECK ORGANIZER.

OUTHAUL A *purchase*, either a *tackle* or a small wire reel winch, to pull the clew of a sail aft along a boom.

PAINTER A short, small line secured to the bow of a small boat for towing or *making fast*. (p. 88)

PAY OUT To let go of a line, or to slack it off. It infers that the rate of easing out is controlled.

PEDESTAL WINCH A winch, used on larger sailboats, with handles mounted on a pedestal above deck. This allows one or two crewmembers to operate the winch while standing up.

PENDANT (Pronounced pennant) A short line permanently spliced to an object for quick hauling, such as a centerboard pendant or a mooring pendant. A short wire used to position a sail, such as a tack pendant. (p. 33)

PENNANT (Also pronounced pennant) A flag whose fly is significantly longer than its hoist, often used to communicate. For example, an answering pennant, or a numeral pennant.

PREVENTER A line used to hold a sail, boom, or yard to a particular setting. A line tautened to prevented a spar, dinghy, or load from moving. A backup for gear under strain. (p. 32)

PURCHASE A *tackle* or device used to increase hauling power.

REEF POINTS Small lines *rove* through grommets in the sail. When the ends are tied with reef knots, they secure the bulk of a reefed sail.

This tackle has four rope parts leading to or from the moving block (at right). Its purchase, or mechanical advantage, is 4:1.

REEVE To run the end of a line through an opening. The past tense is ROVE. See TUCK.

ROPE CLUTCH A mechanical device that grips a rope and holds it under strain. With a lever on top, load may be released instantly. Some models permit gradual release of load. (p. 71)

RUNNING RIGGING All lines and gear used to set and trim sails. See STANDING RIGGING.

SCOPE The ratio of anchor *cable* payed out, compared with the depth of the water. The amount of slack in a line, especially a docking line. (p. 83)

SET FLYING To set a sail attached only at the corners, not fastened along any edge to a *stay* or *spar*.

SHACKLE A small, U-shaped, connecting link often used to join the thimble in an eye splice to a fitting. The open end is closed with a threaded pin. (A snap shackle has a spring-loaded pin.)

SHEAVE (Pronounced shiv) The roller in a *block*, over which the line passes.

SHEET A line or wire rope attached to the lower after corner of a sail (or boom) to control it. The *spinnaker* sheet is the line secured to the clew, which is the opposite corner to the one made fast to the spinnaker pole. See GUY.

SHROUD A wire rope supporting a mast laterally. It is tightened with rigging screws (turnbuckles).

SLATTING The action of slack lines (especially halyards) beating against a mast or spar.

SNATCH BLOCK A single block with a latch in one cheek that opens to receive the bight of a line.

SNUB To hold or check a line which is running out. Usually done by tightening a *turn* or *turns* around a cleat, winch, or bitt.

SOLE The floor of the cockpit or cabin.

SPAR In general, any mast, yard, pole, or boom.

SPINNAKER A light, very large, three-cornered sail set flying forward of all forestays. It is set when the wind is free for running or reaching. (p. 78)

STANCHION(S) The upright posts, usually stainless steel, supporting the lifelines and pulpit rails.

STANDING RIGGING All lines and gear used to support masts and other fixed *spars*.

STAY A wire rope supporting a mast or bowsprit in a fore-and-aft direction. See SHROUD.

SURGE To let the strain off a line intermittently, in a controlled fashion.

STOPPER A short line used to hold another line, or to control it while paying out. (p. 20)

SWAY To haul on the fall of a tackle with the body's weight. Several bodies may be employed. Often used with "up," as in: "Sway up the throat halyard."

SWIG To pull at right angles on the fall of a tackle to gain the last few inches of hoist. In "swigging off" a hal-yard, one crew member pulls hard to the side and suddenly lets go, while another gains the slack created at the belaying pin or cleat. May be repeated to get the last inch of hoist.

TACK (Noun) The lower, for-ward corner of a sail. (p. 32)

TACK (Verb) To come about, that is, to bring the wind from one side to the other by turning the boat into and through the wind.

PORT TACK: Sailing with the wind hitting the port side of the boat first.

STARBOARD TACK: Sailing with the wind hitting the starboard side first.

TACKLE (Pronounced TAY-kul). A means of gain-ing leverage from a line rove through one or more blocks—usually two or more. The number of lines that support the load determine the mechanical advantage. See PURCHASE.

TAIL (Noun) A short synthetic rope spliced to the end of a wire rope (usually a *halyard*) to make handling and securing the wire easier. The tail splice will run through a bock, whereas an eye splice will not.

TAIL (Verb) To haul on a line being heaved in by a winch. Tailing provides the friction that keeps the line from slipping on the drum. (p. 74)

THIMBLE A metal or plastic eye or ring with a raised rim to hold it in place in a rope splice.

TOPPING LIFT A line rigged to support a boom.

TUCK In knot-tying, to insert the end of the line between two other lines or two parts of the same line. In splicing, to insert a strand between two other strands.

TWINE Sailmaker's thread. (p. 59)

TWO-BLOCKED A tackle that has been hauled short, so that the blocks touch.

UNLAY To unwind the strands of a rope, usually in order to work in a splice. (p. 56)

VANG A temporary *tackle* used to hold a boom or gaff in a particular position.

WHIPPING Round turns made with small stuff on the end of a line to prevent it from unlaying. (p. 50)

WORM To wind small stuff in and along the lay (between the strands) of a large rope. Also used in whipping. (p. 85)

Line-Handling Commands

It is embarrassing to hear a command, but not understand what the skipper wants you to do. The better you understand the language of the sea, the more effective a crew member you will be.

But you can't learn it all at once, and in any case the language changes from ship to ship—"Different ships, different long splices," as the old saying puts it. Here, however, is a list of the ten most common line-handling commands to get you started.

TO BELAY—
"Belay mainsheet"—Stop hauling in or paying out, and hold or secure the sheet temporarily by taking one or more Round Turns without making fast. Also used to request a stop to an action.

TO MAKE FAST—
"Make fast jib halyard"—Fasten the halyard securely finishing with a Hitch or a Bend.

TO SECURE—
"Secure boathook"—Stow it away in its proper place. Also often used in place of "Make fast."

TO LET GO—
"Let go mizzen sheet"—Ease off or let a line run as far it will go. "Cast off" is close in meaning to "Let go," but more often used with docking lines.

TO EASE OR TO START—
"Ease the vang six inches"—Pay out slowly a line under stress, but don't necessarily put slack in it.

TO TAKE A STRAIN—
"Take a strain on main boom topping lift"—Haul in on the line so that the slack is taken out of the tackle. The position of the boom, sail, or pole should not be changed.

TO HAUL—
"Haul in spinnaker sheet"—Pull the sheet in by hand, on a single rope or the fall of a tackle.

TO HEAVE—
"Heave in spinnaker guy"—Exert mechanical leverage with a winch, capstan, or marlinespike. Also, to heave a line is to throw it.

TO TRIM—
"Trim genny sheet"—Haul in as far as possible or as far as specifically ordered.

TO OVERHAUL—
"Overhaul mainsheet"—Clear the mainsheet tackle by separating the blocks, so it may be reused.